I Owe God This Praise

Poems by
Deborah Hayman

Words of Inspiration

Isaiah 50:4

The Lord GOD hath given me the tongue of the learned, that I should know how to speak a word in season to him that is weary: he wakeneth morning, by morning, he wakeneth mine ear to hear as the learned.

© 2010 Deborah Hayman
First Edition

All rights reserved.
No part of this publication may be reproduced or transmitted in any form or by any means electronic or mechanical, including photocopy, recording, or any information storage and retrieval system, without permission in writing from both the copyright owner and the publisher.

Requests for permission to make copies of any part of this work should be mailed to:
Permissions Department, Witty Writings Publishing, LLC, 9065 Alsandair Court, Reno, NV 89506

ISBN: 978-1-4276-1907-5

Editing, Typesetting, Cover Image and Design by:
Witty Writings, Inc.
Printed in the United States of America by
Witty Writings Press

Partial funding has been provided by the
Solomon's Temple Church Family of St. Louis, Missouri

Deborah Hayman
Words of Inspiration Ministries
P.O. Box 38542
St. Louis, MO 63138

Dedication

To Demetrius, Jennifer, Jessica, and Demetrius Jr.

Forward

Deborah Johnson Hayman, minister and educator, has provided her readers with an extraordinary collection of poems that powerfully deliver the message of the gospel.

Collectively, this book of poems presents a cross section of the gospel message as sermons, testimonies, prophecies, exhortations and edifications. This menu of poetry has something for everyone.

Clearly, the purpose of this book is to uplift those who may be frustrated or in despair about life's circumstances. It encourages them to hope, persevere, be patient, have faith and trust in God knowing that God has not left them alone.

Finally, she continually reminds the reader that despite life's difficulties, We Owe God Praise.

These poems are rich in Biblical principles designed to build your faith. I highly recommend it to everyone.

Rev. Willie G. Holloway, Sr.
Gospel Power Christian Church
Pastor and Founder

Acknowledgements

First and foremost, I must thank my almighty God and give Him all the praise that's due His name. I would like to thank my mom for her continued support in all I do in the Lord.

Next, I would like to thank Bishop James and Co-Pastor Linda Holloway. Words cannot express the love and respect I have for the both of them.

I would also like to thank my sister Tina, who always comes through for me, and who has been my backbone throughout the entire process of this project.

Thank you Lanita and Mechelle for your much needed help and support. Joyce, Carmen, Cheryl, and MERRI (smile), I love you all. Thank you for letting the Lord use the gifts He has imparted in you to help me with every facet of this project. Jesse P. and Timothy, what can I say, but thank you, thank you, thank you for helping me in more ways than you'll ever know!!

I greatly appreciate and thank Mary for sitting down with me during the beginning stage of this project, and showing me all I needed to know and do to bring my book and CD to its completion. Solomon's Temple, what a wonderful family! Thank you all so very much for your continued support and prayers. I love and appreciated you more than you'll ever know. One cannot ask for a greater spiritual family.

Pastor Willie and Co-Pastor Cecelia Holloway, thank you for your support and prayers.

To my children, Demetrius, Jennifer, and Jessica, and grandson Demetrius Jr., who I love so very much, thank you for your patience and for always understanding how important the work of the Lord is to me.

Finally, count it to my head and not to my heart if I failed to mention anyone. However, I thank you for your support and encouragement in all that you've done to bring this project into completion.

Be Encouraged!

Table of Contents

Title	Page
Are You Ready For Your Miracle	12
You're Too Close Now	14
God Is Getting Ready To Blow My Mind	16
Just A Touch Away	18
I'm Teaching You Something Here	20
Shake It Off, And Let It Go	22
I Got The Can't Help It	24
I Owe God This Praise	26
It's Still Coming	28
I'm Still Here	30
Keep It Up	32
It's Not Coming The Way You Think	34
Get Up And Step In	36
You're Going To Make It Through	38
Just Think, I Almost Quit	40
If He Could, He Would, But He Can't	42
Stump The Devil Down	44
And There's More	46
You Can't Stop This	48
Your Time Has Come To Be	50
You Will Make It Through	52
One More Time	54
You're More Than Meet The Eye	56
Not This Time Satan	58
My Time Is Here	60
Don't Count Me Out	62

Are You Ready For Your Miracle

I'm not asking how you're feeling this morning
Or how long you've been going through
I'm not here today to hold your hand
Or to hear about poor little old you.

But just like the man at the Pool of Bethesda
I'm coming just for you today
If you've been waiting on me and waiting, my children
Watch out, help is on the way.

I just want to know, how do you want it
Two, three, or seven fold
Because I'm here today to bless you, you, and you
So are you ready for your miracle.

Are you ready for your miracle
Yes for me, in your life, to move
Are you ready to let go and let me take control
So your rough road can become smooth.

Yes, are you ready for your miracle
Then all you need to do is believe
Don't tell me this morning what all you're going through
Just reach up my children and receive.

Are you ready for your miracle
Because I'm ready to give it to you
For I see you standing despite the storm
Holding on, no matter what you're going through.

Now you can tell Satan, take that
I'm getting all that belongs to me
For it doesn't matter what I've gone through
God said a new day, I'm about to see.

You might as well give me the praise this morning
Don't wait for the battle is won
You've been in the midnight hour long enough
It's time for you to see the sun.

So are you ready for your miracle
Don't ask me when or where
Just know it won't be long, my children
When people, will have to stop and stare.

They'll say isn't that the one that was so down under
We knew wouldn't get back up
It had to be God that did that thing
Who overflowed even their cup.

Because I'm going to bring you through, my children
Like you've never known before
Opportunities that have been slammed in your faces
I'm going to open even those doors.

So it doesn't matter how you walked in today
And don't be asking Lord, but how
Are you ready for your miracle this morning
Then reach up and take it now.

SCRIPTURE REFERENCE
St. John 5:2-9

You're Too Close Now

Hey, you over there, who is thinking about giving up
Yeah, you too, with your head bowed down
And you right here in front, who can't even praise me
For feeling all wrapped up and bound.

Oh, I had to make a one to one visit this morning
To tell you to hold on to all you've heard
Yes for you, and especially you, my dear loved ones
Because I hear you say I can't take another word.

So I've come to let you know, my children
Before you decide, in this trial, to bow
I'd think twice, if I were you
Because my children, you're too close now.

Oh, you're too close now, to be letting go
In fact, look at all you've been through
Are you going to throw away every pain and heartache
When old things in your life is being made brand new.

For you're too close now
To be thinking about throwing in the towel
Don't let Satan take you out of this
Oh, you can make it this last mile.

Yes, you're too close now
And guess what my children, you do win
So let me gird you with new strength
So you can fight this battle to the end.

Because you're ready to step over the finish line
Oh, my soldiers, if you could only see what I see
You would run all over this church this morning
And nobody could stop you from praising me.

Just think about where you are in this battle
And just how I've already moved for you
Just look at the doors that have already been opened
Can't you see yourself coming on through.

Yes, you're too close now, and you know it
Shame on me, that's what you want to say
For letting the enemy bring me down like that
When I know God's going to make a way.

So are you ready to praise me this morning
For the many breakthroughs that are about to come
Not waiting until these battles are over
Oh, I hear somebody say, I can shout and run.

No, don't let the enemy take your joy from you
For victory is surely yours
So gird yourself up and wipe yourself off
And get ready to walk through your doors.

Oh, I know you were feeling a little low this morning
That's why I had to come down and endow
For I refuse to let you, let your blessings go
Because you're too close now.

SCRIPTURE REFERENCE
2 Kings 7:3-8

God Is Getting Ready To Blow My Mind

I can't speak long on this morning
Because I sense a mighty praise coming on today
For I'm about to finally see some blue skies
Where they had been dark and gray.

For you see, I was just thinking about my problems
And let me tell you, they are more than a few
No, not knowing where to go next in this situation
So I was asking the Lord what else to do.

Then the Lord shot these words down in my spirit
Saying my child, I told you this is your time
Then I had to brace myself, good people
For I saw God getting ready to blow my mind.

Oh, God is getting ready to blow my mind
He's going to show the devil up
Where Satan thought he had me tooth and nail
His little plans are about to erupt.

And God is getting ready to blow my mind
Yes, higher heights, I'm about to go
No more trying to figure it out, my friends
No more being down and low.

Because God is getting ready to blow my mind
Oh, he showed me what's coming to be
Yes, I saw myself moving out of this drought
And what he's going to do, eyes do not see.

So where God is getting ready to take me
Is well worth the wait
And where it seems like God is not going to make it on time
I see him showing up and not being late.

He's getting ready to move for me
In more ways than I ever imagined or thought
He's fighting battles in my life
That I was beginning to think impossible to be fought.

Yes, God is getting ready to blow my mind
And I don't need to tell you when it happens for me
For the way God is about to do this thing
Is big enough for all to see.

So I figure I've talked about my many problems
And what I'm going through long enough
So this is the last time you're going to hear me say
Time for me has been tough.

But I'm standing up in my Savior this morning
Taking my problems by the horn
Letting the devil know this day
God is taking my trials by storm.

Well, it's time for me to move on out of the way, great people
For I've said enough in this rhyme
But if you know that you know, he is talking to you
Look out, God is getting ready to blow your mind.

SCRIPTURE REFERENCE
Job 1:13-19; 2:7-10; 42:1-5, 10-12

Just A Touch Away

I keep reaching for my blessings
But I can't seem to grab a good hold
But I refuse to give up now
As I remember what I've been told.

That this is my time for deliverance
So hold on, I hear, to the end
For no matter how things look now
A great breakthrough God will send.

So I continue to reach out for my deliverance
Knowing it is coming any day
Because he said, it is nigh your door, my child
Yes, it's just a touch away.

Oh, it's just a touch a way
So I have a reason to praise my Lord
No, Satan, you can't make me doubt it
Even if my days are hard.

Because it's just a touch a way
And Lord, I do believe
Oh I expect a mighty move from you, my Savior
Soon a breakthrough, I will receive.

For it's just a touch away
Oh, my doors will open for me
My midnight will soon be over
And sunlight, I will be able to see.

Oh, it's been a long, hard battle, I tell you
Sometimes I was ready to give up
But right in the nick of time
My Savior came in and filled my cup.

He renewed my spirit each time
I thought I could not last
Every time my burdens became overwhelming
I learned my problems, to Him, to cast.

So now it's just a touch a way
No way, will I let go now
For I've come too far, been through too much
For me to bend in this, or bow.

So I'm going to keep on reaching, my Savior
Until I'm able to grab and hold on
I'll say so long to this situation
And good-bye to this storm.

So you don't have to feel sorry for me this morning
Because my deliverance has not yet arrived
For I serve a great and mighty Savior
So I stand firm, knowing I will survive.

And don't think I've lost it either
When you see me grabbing in the air today
But in the spirit I see my breakthrough coming
And it's just a touch away.

SCRIPTURE REFERENCE
St. Matthew 8:3; 9:20-22
St. Luke 6:19

I'm Teaching You Something Here

You want everything to go a certain way
You have plans to work just so
And if they don't go the way you see fit
Boy, can you feel so low.

You don't understand what's going on, you say Jesus
Why aren't my plans working, they're good
I took them to you, my God
Why aren't things going the way they should.

Well, it may just be me, my friends today
But I asked the Lord, please make this clear
Then he said, my child, didn't you know
I'm teaching you something here.

I'm teaching you something here, he told me
For a little higher I need you to go
So come on and go with me
There are some things for you, I need to show.

Oh, I'm teaching you something here
Didn't I hear you say, you'll go all the way
Then you got to learn to move with me
And stop trying to figure out where I'm taking you each day.

Because I'm teaching you something here
Didn't I hear you say, you'll go all the way
Then you got to learn to move with me
And stop trying to figure out where I'm taking you each day.

Because I'm teaching you something here
I want you to totally depend on me
So I'm taking away every dependence you have on you
Then my way only, you'll be able to see.

Yes, you know like I know, my precious child
I've shown you over and over before
That I'm more than able to bring you out
And to open your every door.

And I'm not shorter than my word, oh no
Yes, this too will pass
I will bring you over, bring you through
No, this trial will not last.

But right now, I'm teaching you something here
So you might as well go with the flow
For there are some things I need you to learn
Because there are places you are about to go.

So my child, contrary to the way it seems
Everything is going as plan
It may look like things are out of control
But it's all in my mighty hand.

So shake off that woe is me spirit
And that what if, and what should I do, woe
But let me go on and take you up
Knowing it's all good where ever you go.

Then get all you need to get from me this morning
No this trial, you will not fear
For you now know, I am going to bring you out
But I'm just teaching you something here.

SCRIPTURE REFERENCE
2 Kings 5:1-14

Shake It Off, And Let It Go

God is telling some people to do some things this morning
But you feel like giving up
You're saying every time I try to make a move, God
Things in my life begin to erupt.

But God said, I can't let you go that easy, my children
There's too much in you, I have invested
And I know you can't see it right now either
But when I chose you, I did choose the best.

So before I let you give up your great calling in me
Before I let Satan bring you down low
This is what I want you to do, my soldiers
Shake it off and let it go.

Shake it off and let it go
Shake off all discouragement today
For you should know by now you are in my will
So continue to walk in my way.

Shake it off and let it go
Let go all those worries and doubts
Remembering as you continue to fight for me
I will fight all of your bouts.

Yes, shake it off and let it go
Oh, shake off that woe is me syndrome
Knowing the greater the problems you experience in me
The greater your victory song.

So stand up in your spirit this morning
And say Satan you've hindered me long enough
You've been throwing so much at me lately
That I couldn't see God for dealing with stuff.

But I got too much to do in my Savior
And I'm not going to let you mess up his plan
So I'm going on in my Lord today
While putting all my cares in God's hands.

Yes, I'm going to shake it off and let it go
For my Savior, he does need me
Oh, contrary to what you've been feeding my spirit
God can also use me to make souls free.

So I want to say I'm sorry my Lord Jesus
For almost giving my calling back
Thinking I was this little insignificant soldier
With little power, yes I thought I did lack.

But my God told me, I am somebody
Just like the ones I look up to
Saying, remember it's not them either that do the work
But only in me, my power flow through.

So I'm geared up and ready to run on Jesus
With your strength, no more, will I tell you no
And for anything that's hindering me from obeying your will
I'm shaking it off and letting it go.

SCRIPTURE REFERENCE
Psalm 55:22
St. Matthew 6:25-34
Acts 28:3-5
1 Peter 5:7

I Got The Can't Help It

You have to excuse me this morning
But it's just one of those times
Of when I think about the goodness of Jesus
That wonderful, Savior of mine.

So I need the Lord's strength right now
To keep my feet planted on the ground
Because in any moment I'll be rejoicing
Not caring about how I sound.

Yes, you know how it is, my friends
When you know there's nothing greater than this
Oh, pardon me this morning
For I got the can't help it.

I got the can't help it, yes I do
For my God, my Lord today
So I'm giving you fare warning
Be advised to stay out of my way.

Because I got the can't help it
Praise must come out
Oh, you don't know how long I've suffered
With tears, my God, I sought.

Yes, I got the can't help it
Because He knows just what to do
To let me know each and every time
That I will make it through.

I don't mean to ignore you today
But I owe God so much praise
How much time do you have, my friends
For He has blessed me in so many ways.

He gives me strength from out of no where
And joy from deep within
Loneliness is not in my vocabulary
For he is my closest friend.

Oh, I got the can't help it
Because God continually shows me his love
Opening doors and removing walls
Yes, this can only come from above.

But you better watch out because it's catchy
For it only takes a few
Then there you'll go rejoicing
Remembering what he has done for you.

But enough with all this talk
For I hear God calling my name
Saying, go on and praise me, my child
For you're about to experience a great rain.

Yes, somebody else hears him too
And a great praise is about to hit
Oh, I told you it catches on
Now we all got the can't help it.

SCRIPTURE REFERENCE
Psalm 34:1-3

I Owe God This Praise

Don't be looking at me all funny in here
If you see me break out in a dance today
And don't worry, I haven't lost it either
Just move on out the way.

Because you don't know where God has brought me from
For I haven't had time to tell it all
How he keeps on picking me up, my friends
And just won't let me fall.

So it's bubbling way down in my spirit today
So my friends don't be amazed
When it looks like I just can't help myself
Because I owe God this praise.

Oh, I owe God this praise
For he's always bringing me out
When it looks like this time I won't make it
Another battle again, he's fought.

Yes, I owe God this praise this morning
Because it's he who sees me through
When I'm feeling worn out, and down in the dumps
He makes me feel brand new.

So I owe God this praise today
And no devil will take my joy
Because I owe him for all he's done for me
That's why I can't sit here and be coy.

Yes, my friends, I must pick them up and put them down
For God is the keeper of my soul.
So I can't act all humble and lowly today
But I must stand up and be bold.

And let the devil know, I see your works
But that won't turn me away
From all the things God has promised me
So I must continue to bless him today.

Because I owe God this praise, this morning
For every test and every trial God's won
And I have a right to give him all that's due his name
Dance, shout, clap, and even run.

So I don't mean to ignore you this morning
But God has blessed me so
That when I should be feeling all down and out
My spirit man keeps shouting no.

Look at all you've been through, it says to me
From nowhere, look where you are now
So I dare you give up on your Lord and Savior
Not now, you will not bow.

So excuse me for just a minute, if you will
Or just come on and join in this craze
For this is the time to let go and let God
For we owe God this praise.

SCRIPTURE REFERENCE
2 Samuel 6:12-21

It's Still Coming

Just dropping a few words in your spirit
To give you what God said
To encourage some discouraged hearts
That it's true, what you have read.

You were excited when you first heard it
God said it, it must be true
But it's amazing as time goes on
What trials can sometimes do.

But God is telling someone today
Get up, continue running
For the blessings he promised you
Rejoice, it's still coming.

It's still coming, yes it is
If God said it, it will come to be
Whether it's new cars or new homes
Or families being made free.

It's still coming, God said it
That healing he promised you
More money, a new job
Delivering your souls too.

Oh, it's still coming
That problem that will not cease
God's going to calm that storm
In the midst, there will be peace.

But you don't know my problem, you're saying
And the toll it's taking on me
But God knows all, my friends in Christ
And deliverance, you'll also see.

And he's going to bring you up and out
He knows how much you can bear
It may seem as though he's nowhere to be found
But for you, our Lord, does care.

So yes, it's still coming
You thought it was over for sure
Throw in the towel, I don't think so
But continue in God to endure.

Oh I know you thought it should be here by now
What's taking God so long
But the greater the trial, the greater the blessing
So hold on for your victory song.

For we won't be able to contain you then
A testimony, you'll try to give
But all we'll see is your praising our Lord
Shouting, I know that Jesus lives.

Oh God sees you're gearing up now
Saying beware Satan, I'm still in the running
Yes, I thought it was over, but no, not now
Because God said, it's still coming.

SCRIPTURE REFERENCE
St John 11:1-7, 11, 17, 20-35, 38-44

I'm Still Here

I know we're in need of a blessing
And a breakthrough in God would do us good
I also know we're still trying to get things right
No, we're not all the way in there, like we should.

Ok, maybe I'm just talking about myself this morning
Maybe everybody else got it all going on
But sometimes I felt like I couldn't take it any longer
So many trials, making me feel so worn.

But you see, this morning I have to praise my blessed Savior
For when I thought I was losing it, he spoke in my ear
That's why I can stand this day and say through it all, my Lord
Because of you, I'm still here.

I'm still here, hoping and believing
Though Satan tried to cause me to doubt
Giving me more strength to run on
As he reminded me of the other battles he fought.

Oh, I'm still here
And I'm getting stronger day by day
When I thought it was all over, God just take me home
He said, it's not time my child, I need you to stay.

Yes, I'm still here
For God kept me when I couldn't keep myself
He carried me on through this battle
When I had no strength in him left.

You see, God knows how to bring you up
When you feel lower than low can get
He knows just how to encourage your hearts
As your walls close in, teaching you not to fret.

Oh, enough with the downer, this morning
I got to praise my God today
For he took all my hurt, heartache, and pain
And said, my child, everything is ok.

So I'm still here
For God knew just what to do
I can look at my trials and tests a little differently now
Knowing through it all, God will bring me through.

Oh, I thank you Jesus for your mercy
For you didn't give in to my pain
When Satan thought he was taking my mind
You said not here, my child is still sane.

So excuse me, but I owe God something today
For he didn't give up on me
But he kept working on me and pouring in his strength
Until my spirit again became free.

Oh, I feel like praising my Savior this morning
So if you're near me when I start, just stay clear
Because Satan thought he had me down for the count
But praise God, I'm still here.

SCRIPTURE REFERENCE
Psalm 61:1-4; 62:2, 8

Keep It Up

I'm not talking to my complainers
Or to those who still yet doubt
I'm not talking to my forgetful ones
Quickly forgetting the battles, I fought.

And I'm not talking to my unfaithful
Those I ask repeatedly before they move
Nor to those with little or no faith
Not believing, if their paths aren't smooth.

But to those who have been waiting
Still believing their breakthrough will erupt
I'm talking to you today, my loved ones
Just three words, keep it up.

Keep it up, I'm here to yet encourage you
That help is on the way
Soon, very soon, my children
You'll see a brighter day.

Just keep it up, don't stop believing
For your time is here, is now
So tell Satan, you won't give up
And you won't bend or bow.

But keep it up, keep praising me
Knowing, I do hear your cry
While remembering I've never forsaken you
So in this trial, you will not die.

Oh my children, I see you yet rejoicing
Believing victory has come to be
And I see you giving me glory
Even though deliverance you still don't see.

That's why Satan is trying with all his might
To cause you to back down
He's raising our fires hotter than hot
Trying to change your smiles to frowns.

But keep it up, it is your season
Your change has truly come
Don't worry how I'm doing it
For you can't see where I'm coming from.

But I'm coming like a whirlwind
A mighty move you are about to see
And when it's all said and done
All will know it came from me.

You just keep doing what you're doing
Knowing it's touching my heart
That you can still yet praise me
Like you've been doing from the start.

So if you start wondering, what's going on here
If things seem mighty tough
Just remember your time is truly here
So my faithful, keep it up.

SCRIPTURE REFERENCE
Psalm 37:4, 7
Isaiah 1:19

It's Not Coming The Way You Think

You keep looking in other directions, my children
Then you get all upset with me
But you're looking in all the wrong places
That's why your deliverances, you can't see.

So I've come to pay you a little visit
To let you know, I'm still here
But I need you to listen good right now
For a change in your thinking, it'd steer.

Yes I'll deliver you, my people, this morning
By my power, no, you won't sink
Yes, I'm going to do all I said I'll do
But it's not coming the way you think.

No, it's not coming the way you think
But a breakthrough is definitely yours
So let go and let me do the work for you
So I can help you walk through your doors.

But it's not coming the way you think
That's why you keep bumping against the wall
No, I didn't tell you I was moving that way
And I didn't tell you to do some things at all.

Oh, it's not coming the way you think
So are you ready to go with me
Then you must step out, having faith in my word
For my moves, you won't be able to see.

Yes my children, now it's time for you to trust me
And to take me at my word
You've been listening, holding on, and getting prayed for
Now step out on what all you've heard.

Yes, I told you good things are about to happen for you
And my word, my children, it doesn't lie
Blessings are ready to rain down on my people
So stop looking with your natural eye.

Because it's not coming the way you think
So stop looking at ways that make sense
For your blessings are too big to be boxed in
So let me out of your fence.

For you got too much coming, my children
And I'm meeting all your needs
For when you didn't have much of anything
I saw you planting and sowing those seeds.

Now it's time for your harvest to come forth
It's time to reap all that you've sown
So get ready my children, yes move with me
And watch me right your wrongs.

So now I ask you, are you ready for your miracles
Well, you're standing right at the brink
But remember, keep your eyes and focus completely on me
Because it's not coming the way you think.

SCRIPTURE REFERENCE
Deuteronomy 28:1, 2
2 Kings 5:1-14
Proverbs 3:5, 6
Isaiah 55:8, 9

Get Up And Step In

I've been telling you this is your season
I've been saying your time has come
But somebody is still looking around
Wondering where is it coming from.

So let me bring it to you again, my soldiers
Because I love you, my children, so
Then when I tell you to move, listen good
I just want you to go.

Don't worry about how I'm going to do it
Or think how your chances are so thin
But when I tell you the water is troubling
Then get up and step in.

Oh get up and step in
For the angels are at the pool
All you need to do is get in there
It's no time to act suave or cool.

But get up and step in
For your season is nigh, it's here
So shake off all doubt right now
And rebuke any and all fear.

Yes, get up and step in
Take it, if you have to, by force
For it's your blessing, it belongs to you
So no need to feel any remorse.

I can't tell you enough, my children
You better move while the moving is here
Don't be like the man at the Pool of Bethesda
Who didn't recognize me when I came near.

But started telling me what he couldn't do
Many excuses, he began to unfold
Even though I came to him personally
And asked do you want to be made whole.

So I'm saying this morning, Get up and step in
If you want to be made whole today
If you need me to move for you
If you need blessings to come your way.

And what's so good about this stirring, my children
It's not just for the first one who steps in
But for those who have been seeking me and holding on
This troubling of the water, for you, I send.

So don't tell me about what you don't have
Or keep asking, what are you going to do
For I'm not asking you how badly you feel this morning
Or how terribly, you're going through.

Yes listen good, I've come to ask you once more
Are you ready, in this battle, to win
If you're saying, yes Lord, do it for me
Then get up and step in.

SCRIPTURE REFERENCE
St. John 5:2-9

You're Going To Make It Through

Someone is saying, I'm going through this morning
So I don't want to hear any of that
All I want to know today
Is where is my deliverance at.

For I've been waiting for a long time
And I see no change at all
They keep telling me to step forward
But I keep running into a wall.

Well, it's time for some encouragement this morning
Because God knows you'll make it through
You're going to get all the blessings, my friends today
That our God has promised you.

Yes, the storm may be turbulent
And the wind ever so strong
You may be feeling so low to the ground
And you're thinking, what is a victory song.

But our God said it is coming
All that he said is due
So he came to assure you this morning
That you're going to make it through.

Yes, you're going to make it through, he's saying
For there is nothing too great or strong
For our God with his mighty power
Can right any and every wrong.

Oh you're going to make it through
For God is going to see to that
And you won't be able to sit long today
Because he's meeting you where you're at.

Yes, you're going to make it through
So tell discouragement, you have to flee
For God's word will accomplish this morning
What he's set forth for you and me.

For he said, my children, oh they need me
For despair is taking its toll
But I can't let them give up now
When victory is about to unfold.

So I must come down to minister
To encourage them to hold on
For some think they won't make it
Through their rough and rugged storm.

But it's not over until I say so
And it can't end until you win
So it's time to rise up this morning
And say Satan I refuse to bend.

Oh, you almost had me for a moment
Had me wondering what to do
But now I know, so I'm praising my God
For I'm going to make it through.

SCRIPTURE REFERENCE
Psalm 3:1-7

Just Think, I Almost Quit

Have you ever been so down, so low
That you can't reach up and touch the ground
God, I'm doing all I know to do, you say
But still no help can be found.

Please no more sermons about it today
And don't tell me, I just need to stand
But God always knows just what to say
So get ready, his anointed band.

For just when I was ready to throw in the towel
And say, God, I'm sorry, but that's it
He said, not today, I'm depending on you
And just think, I almost quit.

Just think, I almost quit
But then God said, haven't I been there for you
So one more time, just step out for me
And watch what I will do.

Just think, I almost quit
Then God came down from on high
And said, I hear a desperate call from my discouraged child
I must answer my soldier's cry.

Just think, I almost quit
But then God, he ministered to my heart
Saying, I will never leave or forsake you, my child
I'm still with you, as from the start.

Then he began to comfort me through and through
Like only my Lord can do
Lifting me up in my spirit
Making me feel brand new.

I said, God I think I can make it now
Since I've had this talk with you, Lord
My problems, they don't seem as bad as they did
My situation doesn't look that hard.

And just think, I almost quit
But God is good, isn't he
He won't let the devil eat you all up
But he'll put you back where you should be.

Oh, I'm ready again to meet my challenges
For God said, he allowed them to be
He said he knew I could take it, yes he did
That's why he gave these trials to me.

And when it's all over, said, and done
He can let the devil know
I told you my child loved me for me
So you might as well let it go.

And don't think you're going through this for naught, he said
Remember Job got more than a little bit
And like him, doors are ready to open for you
And just think, I almost quit.

SCRIPTURE REFERENCE
Jeremiah 20:7-13
1 Corinthians 16:13

If He Could, He Would, But He Can't

Satan's been trying to knock me down
To pull me out of the race
But try what he will, he can't stop me
He can only slow up my pace.

Because I've been bought with a price
And my price is too much to let go
That's why I must continue on in my Jesus
It doesn't matter the valley, or how low.

Yes, I'm still yet standing on his word this morning
No, Satan didn't cause me to faint
And I know he won't win this battle
Yes, if he could, he would, but he can't.

Oh if he could, he would, but he can't
No, joy I can't let him take
But I lift my hands to Jesus this day
And a joyful noise, I'll continue to make.

For if he could, he would, but he can't
He can't take my peace from me
Because I know I will make it through this trial
That's why I yet hope, though deliverance I don't see.

Oh if he could, he would, be he can't
He can't stop God's mighty move
It doesn't matter the picture painted before me
My heart in God is still soothed.

That's why I'm not crying this morning
For I know God's got things under control
Or for me to act like I can't make it
When God told me things are about to unfold.

Yes, it is my time, and I know it
And I'm not taking it back
I don't care what the enemy is doing right now
Or how, in this situation, he acts.

For if he could, he would, but he can't
He can't take my deliverance from me
Yes, I'm getting all that my God has promised
For I know what he said, will be.

That's why I must praise God today
For all I have in store
Knowing the more I lift up my precious Savior
The closer I get to my door.

Yes it was a battle, but I made it here
So I refuse to sit down on the Lord
But I'm going to give him all of me
With my God, we'll be on one accord.

Oh, Satan thought he'd quiet me this morning
Because of my trials, I'll be sad and quaint
Thought that even this storm could stop my praise
Yes if he could, he would, but he can't.

SCRIPTURE REFERENCE
Exodus 15:6
Psalm 41:11
St. Luke 10:19
Acts 28:3-5

Stump The Devil Down

I know you're not going to praise God this morning
For I saw what all you did
Can't get it right at all, he said to you
So you should have buried yourself, yes and hid.

Oh, don't you dare let the devil get the best of you
For you know what he's all about
And he knows you're not only stepping through your door
But your battles are near about fought.

So guess what you're going to do on this blessed day in God
You're going to make heavenly sounds
You're going to shout and lift up your hands to Jesus
Oh you're going to stump the devil down.

You're going to stump the devil down this morning
Yes, who is he, to stop you from praising your Lord
Show him this trial may be rough right now
But you're not complaining about life being so hard.

Instead, you're going to stump the devil down in here
Showing God you still yet believe
Oh yes, you hit a bump or two in the road this week
But God's deliverance, you will receive.

So go ahead, stump the devil down this day
Yes, shake all woe and gloom off of you
And say, God I may not be where I want to be
But I'm better than before, that's true.

Yes God sees, it's not enough going through trials and battles
But then your faults, Satan tries to amplify
But tell him, I got news for you devil
That's where grace for me, God will magnify.

Because the Lord told me a long time ago
I don't love you, my child, because you're so great
But what makes me proud of you my soldier
Is when you continue to hold on to me by faith.

Oh let's stump the devil down this morning
For trying to stop your praise
You know your breakthroughs are already coming
And look out, they're coming in so many ways.

Yes, God knew you felt like hiding away this morning
And he knows just what we need
So he's here today just to strengthen some hearts
So tell Satan, you better take heed.

And rise up in our Savior this morning
And yes he said, make your request known
For he knows Satan said, you might as well let it all go
But God said, not so, that's all wrong.

Oh yes, our time is now, great people of God
So let's make the enemy frown
And stand to our feet and praise our God
Oh, let's stump the devil down.

SCRIPTURE REFERENCE
Malachi 4:3
Romans 16:20

And There's More

Sometimes I see you stopping
In the mist of your trials and tests
And begin thanking me, your God and Savior
For giving you peace and rest.

For Lord, where would I be, you'll say
If it was not for you
No way could I survive this
No way could I make it through.

Because my children, I see you praising me
For the opening of your every door
I've come today to let you know
Continue on, for there's more.

There's more for you my faithful
Who, through it all, is continuing to be true
Who against all hope in your situation
Is still expecting me to bring you through.

There's more, I just stopped by to tell you
So reach for the stars, I say
Ask largely, my precious ones
And let me have my way.

There's more, and you sense it too
But you're thinking this could not be
All these wonderful blessing Savior
My mind is playing tricks on me.

But let me speak to you, my children
Let me tell you that it's true
Because you dared to trust my word
No matter what was happening to you.

I see you in the midnight hour
And when the rain is pouring down
I'm touched by your tender tears
And you refused to wear a frown.

Yes, I have been blessing mightily
I have loosed many and made free
But to my faithful, it's not over yet
There's more and you'll soon see.

So yes, I've been delivering
And I've opened many doors
But eyes have not seen, dear ones
What all you have in store.

So continue to lift me up
Even in the midst of your storm
Continue to hold dear my word
Knowing Satan can't do you any harm.

Because not only will you receive
What you believe you have in store
For yes, blessings cometh, my precious ones
Those blessings and there's more.

SCRIPTURE REFERENCE
Deuteronomy 28:2
Isaiah 64:4

You Can't Stop This

I'm going up in my Jesus
And there's no turning me around
My mind is set, my dear friends today
Yes, my feet are planted on solid ground.

Because God keeps telling me this is my season
My time to be blessed
My time to find total contentment
To have, in him, peace and rest.

So it doesn't matter what I'm facing this morning
And I got a long, and I mean, long list
Because God is going to do what he said he would
And devil, you can't stop this.

No Satan, you can't stop this
You can't stop God's great plans for me
For he told me, yes you paid the price, my child
And now it's time for you to be made free.

So no, you can't stop this
So it doesn't matter what you bring my way
I'm still going to hold on to what my Jesus says
As I wait patiently for my blessed day.

Oh, you can't stop this
For I'm getting my great reward
Yes, I've learned how to hold out in my Jesus
And to walk on one accord.

Oh yes, this has been a horrific battle
One that would make a strong saint cry
But I thank God for my sweet Jesus
Who still didn't pass me by.

But he encouraged me through my dark hours
Whispering continually, hold on to my word
Wait, I say on my promises
And you will receive all you've heard.

So now, devil, you can't stop this
Because my deliverance is nigh my door
And I'm ready to walk in this morning
To receive all I have in store.

I know some thought I wouldn't make it
Others even assumed I would fall
But God is coming through for me
Changing the speech of them all.

So if you're wondering why I'm praising him today
It's because I'm receiving my blessings as they come
So make a path for me, will you please
If you see me break out and run.

Yes devil, you thought you shot me down with this trial
But again, I tell you, you missed
Because God is getting ready to bless me good
And you can't stop this.

SCRIPTURE REFERENCE
Exodus 14:5-31

Your Time Has Come To Be

I wanted to go somewhere differently, I tell you
But the Lord wouldn't let me be
All I could hear him say this morning was
My child, you are indeed free.

So I make no apologies this day
For God is still in control
Oh he keeps saying don't worry about your situation
For true deliverance is about to unfold.

And what's so good about my Savior, my friends
Is what he's doing doesn't apply only to me
So I challenge you to grab on to what he's telling you today
Because your time has come to be.

Oh your time has come to be, God said it
So don't worry about your problems today
For he said, I heard you when you called me
So know that help is on the way.

And your time has come to be
He said continue to instill these words in you
For the enemy has turned up the fire, I know it
Trying to keep you from making it through.

But remember your time has come to be
So let no devil take what's yours
But gird up your minds this morning
That you will walk through your victory doors.

God said he had to come to encourage hearts this morning
Because somebody is about to let go
And somebody else can't see their blessings
Because their spirits are oh so low.

But the devil is a liar this morning
The more he fights, the more you know it's yours
So start speaking those things that be not
As you receive all that is in store.

Because your time has come to be
No, you have no sad song
I know everything seems to be going awry
But hold on, it won't be long.

Because I'm moving in the spirit as I speak, my children
Restoring all that was lost
So when the enemy comes to you shouting his bluff
Remind him who's the boss.

For I take pleasure in taking the worst situation
Turning it all around
So if you think you're sinking fast this morning
You're about to be planted on solid ground.

So come on, give me the glory
No, it doesn't matter what you see
For I'm right now moving for you, you, and you
Yes, your time has come to be.

SCRIPTURE REFERENCE
Hebrews 6:13-15

You Will Make It Through

It may seem like all is lost sometimes
Your trials, it just won't end
You may even be taunted with thoughts
That this fight, you just can't win.

Yes, the fire is raging hot
The flames are ever so high
But when Satan finishes his bluff
Remember, he is a lie.

Oh, he can make it look disastrous
We agree this to be true
But when it's all said and done, my friends
You will make it through.

You will make it through
Yes, this trial too, will pass
No matter how deep your valley
Your troubles will not last.

And you will make it through
For God will bring you out
Remembering each and every battle
For you, our Savior has fought.

So you will make it through
No, his word cannot fail
It won't be long, when you again
Will have another story to tell.

For God see you in your desert
He hears your cries for help
That's why he has you in his arms
Oh, in him you're being kept.

You'll make it through, he's saying
No, I won't let you fall
No matter how wide the mountain
No matter how tall the wall.

For I will give you new strength, I hear him
When weakness takes its toll
When sadness tries to overtake you
My joy in you will unfold.

Peace will be your covering
Faith will be your shield
When Satan with his last efforts
Comes in for the kill.

And you will rise up in boldness, he said
Believing what I'm saying today
Against hope you will stand in me
Though you still don't see a way.

And when others see you yet rejoicing
They'll wonder, what's wrong with you
But you'll say, I may not be there yet
But I will make it through.

SCRIPTURE REFERENCE
Acts 27:13-44

One More Time

Do you ever feel that some times
You're at the end of your rope
You know what God can do, my friends
But in this battle, you see no hope.

Crying out to our precious Savior
Oh yes, he heard your every prayer
And when you said, Lord though I've been trying to hold on
It's more than I can bear.

Well, the Lord has a word today, my friends
And it's especially for you
For he knows you have it down in you
To see this trial all the way through.

So one more time, he is saying
Go forth and dare to believe
Don't give up on me now, my children
But hold out until deliverance is received.

One more time, speak to your mountain
And command that it be removed
Don't let go until all rough edges
Straighten up and become smooth.

One more time, lift me up
And praise my holy name
Believing if you do it
No, you won't be the same.

For I know your situations
And I see your hurts and pains
I know that even right now, my children
All you see is rain.

But look back at the trials if you will
Where I have brought you from
And what all I put down in you
Giving you more strength to run.

So don't give up now, my warriors
When victory is a reach a way
But one more time, do it for me
Dare to wait on your promises today.

One more time, you'll say, I'll do it
Knowing deliverance is at my door
So why should I let it all go now
When there's so much I have in store.

So I'll wait on your promises Lord
For you placed them in my heart
And I'll be as strong in my faith for you Jesus
As I was in the start.

Yes, I was feeling quite weary this morning
For there was no more strength, I could find
But Lord just for you, I'll go back in
And fight one more time.

SCRIPTURE REFERENCE
1 Samuel 1:2-20
St. Mark 8:22-25

You're More Than Meet The Eye

Yes, you my precious children
It's you that I choose
With you doing the job
There's no way I will lose.

I know you're asking, who me
Who me you're talking to
The one who sometimes doubt you
Thinking no way I'll make it through.

Yes, it's you who I speak of
Don't you know who you are
You're more than meet the eye
You're my chosen, yes by far.

You're more than meet the eye
The powers inside you possess
You know where to find victory
Yes through my word, you know success.

You're more than meet the eye
You're holding on to receive
The blessings I promised just for you
Against hope, you still believe.

You're more than meet the eye
You praise and worship my name
You know because of my precious word
You're no longer, my children, the same.

And you're learning, oh my children
To totally depend on me
You're daring to trust my word
Knowing only I can make you free.

You strive oh to please me
It hurts you when you fall
But each time you're getting better
You're moving quicker when I call.

Your heart towards me is opened
Lord use me, I hear you say
So I've come to encourage your heart
Go forward my children today.

For you're more than meet the eye
I know your particular storms
Remember I was there
When each of them was formed

But you're more than a conqueror
You're the apples of my eye
I have chosen you my mighty warriors
To lift my word up high.

I know you feel unworthy
And sometimes you ask me why
But again I say go forward
For you're more than meet the eye.

SCRIPTURE REFERENCE
Deuteronomy 10:15
1 Peter 2:9

Not This Time Satan

It's a new dawn this morning
I can feel it in the air
Trying to maintain my composure
Not trying to cause people to stare.

For you see, when I woke up this morning
Satan tried his tricks once more
Had me worn down, oh just beat down
Before I could make it through the doors.

But new strength emerged from heaven
And my mind, yes God renewed
So I say, not this time Satan
I'm in a different kind of mood.

Not this time Satan
You won't stop God's plan for me
I'm going on through this trial
Holding on till he makes me free.

Oh, not this time Satan
You won't make me feel blue
For God, he will do it for me
So I tell you what I'm going to do.

I'm going to lift my hands to heaven
I'm going to give my God some praise
I'm going to thank him for his goodness
For blessing me in so many ways.

So not this time Satan
You may have gotten to me in the past
But a new commitment I made to the Lord
And this time I mean for it to last.

I'm ready to run on, my Jesus
I'm ready to do your will
No more wondering what went wrong
No more standing still.

Lord, give me wings this morning
Because I'm ready to take off and fly
Yes, I still have some problems
But I've already had my cry.

For Lord you've been too good to me
Even when I'm not doing my best
You never once turned your back on me
You didn't love me any less.

So I refuse on this day Satan
To let you get the best of me
Because my soul is filled with God's joy
My mind is indeed free.

I better move on out this morning
Yes, God is ready to have his way
So I say again, not this time Satan
I'm going to praise my Savior today.

SCRIPTURE REFERENCE
Jonah 1:1-5, 15-17; 2:1-10; 3:1-4

My Time Is Here

I heard it through the preached word of God
I even read what the Lord had to say
Then time again I'd hear from his servants
That deliverance is coming my way.

But the more I'd hear it, God's people
It seemed the worse my situation would get
I didn't know what to do at one point
So I prayed, God, I can't see help in this pit.

Then the light clicked on in my spirit
As I heard, the way out is up, so don't fear
Yes, everyone has been telling you, but you must also see
That my child, your time is here.

My time is here, he said, say it
Until it gets down in your soul
Continue to speak those things that be not
Yes, stand up in me and be bold.

My time is here, but do you believe it
Do you see what I see, my child
For there is a storm of blessings coming your way
And let me tell you, it won't be mild.

My time is here, then I said it
Until I could see what he was showing me
Hey, God is delivering me, and right now
So back off Satan, for now I see.

Yes, you can go through so much, my friends of God
That your spirit can become numb
I hear everything they're saying, you think
But I've grown too tired to run.

But because God is who he is in our lives
He always steps right in on time
And where you were feeling like throwing in the towel
In your Lord, total peace you'd find.

Oh my time is here, you can also say
Yes, God I see it too now
I must go through this to receive my prize
So I can't let go, I can't bow.

Yes, I must refuse to give up on my Jesus
For I come too far to miss out
For God has been telling me, it's mine for the taking
So take away, Lord, any and all doubt.

Then gird me up in my spirit, dear Lord
To go after all you promised me
Not dwelling on what all I'm facing today
But to see it the way you see.

So excuse me on this morning, great people
If you see me shout or shed a tear
For I can see this thing for myself, I do
Now I know my time is here.

SCRIPTURE REFERENCE
Exodus 3:15-17; 5:1-9, 19-23; 6:1; 14:21-31

Don't Count Me Out

So you think I'm not going to make it
Yes, I know things look pretty rough
Oh, my problems are out there and you see it
And my situation is quite tough.

Then when I think it's almost over
And a final breakthrough is near
Here comes Satan with another blast of trouble
Trying to instill in me much fear.

But I got news for Satan this morning
This may look like a defeated bout
But remember, I still have Jesus on my side
So oh no, don't count me out.

Don't count me out
Because I'm still standing on God's word
Yes, I'm going to believe my Savior to the end
Holding onto everything I've heard.

So don't count me out
And don't feel sorry for me
For this trial is bringing me closer to my God
While in my spirit, he's making me free.

So don't count me out
Instead watch what God will do
As I continue to trust and hope in him
My God, he will bring me through.

So I do have a reason to praise him this morning
As I think about what he's already done
Bringing me out when I saw no way
Giving me strength time after time, to run.

So I know, for this thing, God will do it
He's going to bring me out of this mess
And where Satan has caused stress and confusion
God's going to give me complete peace and rest.

So don't count me out
But if you would, rejoice with me
Because before long I'll also be able tell a story
On how my Savior made me free.

Yes, I know some situations are so horrific
That it seems not even God can fix this thing
But when I think about what he brought me through last time
My heart begins to rejoice and sing.

So I don't have time to feel sorry for myself
As though this battle is already lost
Where my Savior, my God, is still boss.

Yes, I'm going to praise God through this trial
You see that's what I've been taught
For I know when it's all said and done, I got the victory
So don't count me out.

SCRIPTURE REFERENCE
2 Samuel 22:3
Judges 16:21, 22, 25-30
Psalm 18:2, 3
Acts 27:25

Words of Inspiration Ministries
P.O. Box 38542
St. Louis, MO 63138

www.wordsofinspiration.net

www.ingramcontent.com/pod-product-compliance
Lightning Source LLC
LaVergne TN
LVHW051710080426
835511LV00017B/2829